Desert Hiking Tips

Expert Advice on Desert Hiking and Driving

Bruce Grubbs

HELENA, MONTANA

A FALCON GUIDE®

Falcon® is continually expanding its list of recreational guidebooks. All books include detailed descriptions, accurate maps, and all the information necessary for enjoyable trips. You can order extra copies of this book and get information and prices for other Falcon® guidebooks by writing Falcon, P.O. Box 1718, Helena, MT 59624 or calling toll-free 1-800-582-2665. Please ask for a free copy of our current catalog. Visit our website at www.falconguide.com.

Printed in Canada.

1 2 3 4 5 6 7 8 9 0 TP 03 02 01 00 99 98

Cover Photo by Kerrick James.

Library of Congress Cataloging-in-Publication Data
Grubbs, Bruce (Bruce O.)
Desert hiking tips : field-tested wisdom on desert hiking and driving / Bruce Grubbs.
p. cm. — (A FalconGuide)
Includes bibliographical references (p.).
ISBN 1-56044-818-0 (pbk. : alk. paper)
1. Desert survival—Guidebooks. 2. Hiking —Guidebooks. 3. Backpacking—Guidebooks. 4. All terrain vehicle driving—Guidebooks. 5. Hiking—Southwest, New—Guidebooks. 6. Backpacking—Southwest, New—Guidebooks. 7. All terrain vehicle driving—Southwest, New—Guidebooks. 8. Southwest, New—Guidebooks.
I. Title. II. Series: Falcon guide.
GV200.5.G78 1999
613.6'9—dc21

98-36952
CIP

CAUTION

Outdoor recreation can be dangerous, including hiking and backpacking. Everyone who goes into the wilderness or backcountry assumes some risk and responsibility for his or her own actions and safety.

The information contained in this book is a summary of the author's personal experiences, research, review of existing literature on desert hiking. However, neither this book (nor any other book) can assure your safety from the elements. Nor can this book (or any other book) replace sound judgment and good decision-making skills, which will greatly reduce the risks of going into the wilderness.

Learn as much as possible from this book and other sources of information, prepare for the unexpected, and be cautious. The reward will be a safer and more enjoyable experience.

 Text pages printed on recycled paper.

Contents

Acknowledgments

After more than 30 years of desert hiking, I would like to thank the many people who shared their ideas and techniques with me. Most will have to remain unnamed, but I want to single out a few. At the top of the list is Bill Sewrey, who was a mentor and an inspiration to an entire generation of Arizona hikers. I especially wish to thank Jean Rukkila for an excellent job of proofreading and for her many suggestions and tips. Many thanks go to Russ Schneider, my editor, for working with me to make a collection of ideas into a book. Thank you to Erin Turner and all the other folks at Falcon Publishing for their great work. Finally, heartfelt thanks to Duart Martin for encouraging and supporting this project every step of the way.

Introduction

A *desert* is usually defined as a region that receives less than 10 inches of annual precipitation; however, the practical definition of desert for the backcountry traveler is any area where the availability of water dominates the trip. Many mountain ranges fall into this definition of desert, so the tips in this book apply there also. In addition, deserts can be divided into hot and cold— the Sonoran Desert of southern Arizona is a classic hot desert, while the Great Basin desert of northern Nevada is a cold desert. Winter snow is rare in hot deserts but summer temperatures often reach 110 degrees F. When hiking in summer, choose routes that follow streams, such as slot canyon descents that require continuous wading or swimming. Cold deserts, on the other hand, commonly do see some snowfall during the winter months, and the summer heat is not as extreme. Winter hiking in high deserts may become more like winter mountaineering, which requires skills beyond the scope of this book.

This book focuses primarily on backcountry travel in the Great American Desert, which includes most of Arizona, New Mexico, Utah, and Nevada, as well as portions of Colorado, California, Oregon, and Idaho. However, many of the techniques and much of the equipment recommended in this book may be useful for hikers in well-watered regions, as well as other desert regions of the world.

Spring, fall, and winter are the best desert hiking seasons, though summer can be enjoyable if you are properly prepared. You should carefully consider any desert trip in midsummer. Breakdowns, dried-up water sources and other pitfalls can turn a hot-season trip into a deadly vacation.

Throughout this book, I discuss a lot of the risks and dangers associated with desert travel, and you may get the idea that the desert is an unfriendly place to hike. Nothing could be further from the truth. With some knowledge and a few precautions, the desert is an inviting place to explore and may become more addicting than any forested mountain wilderness.

Desert Tips

TRIP PLANNING

Leave your itinerary with a responsible person (preferably a friend or family member) who will call the appropriate rescue authority (local sheriff, Bureau of Land Management, National Park Service, or USDA Forest Service) if you are overdue. This is critical for solo trips but important even when traveling with a group.

Remember: **Always notify your responsible person as soon as you return,** to avoid a costly and unnecessary search attempt.

Be sure **everyone in the group knows the trip plan,** including the approach route and meeting points if more than one vehicle will be used. If the group intends to separate on the hike, make sure each has a copy of the map, trip plan, and a set of car keys.

Don't hike solo in the desert, especially in remote areas or hot weather, unless you are experienced. Even then, plan and hike more cautiously than you would with a group.

Hiking and backcountry **guidebooks** can be a valuable source of specific information. They are especially useful when you explore a new area for the first time.

Before planning a desert hiking trip, **check with the government agency** having jurisdiction over the area. Rangers can often provide you with up-to-date road, trail, and water information, as well as information on where to find maps.

Don't rely exclusively on information from a **person you don't know.** Check his or her knowledge by asking a question to which you already know the answer. Such care is especially important when gathering information about water sources.

MAPS

Maps are essential for desert trip planning and route finding during the hike. Trails are rare in many areas, and those that are shown on the maps may be little used, faint, and hard to find.

Topographic atlases that cover an entire state are also helpful for an overview of an area and finding roads to the trailhead. However, some atlases do not accurately portray back roads, and unmaintained roads are abandoned frequently. Use caution.

USDA Forest Service and Bureau of Land Management maps usually don't show terrain features. However, they are excellent road maps. Back roads are shown as maintained, unmaintained, and four-wheel drive on most of these maps.

Agency road numbers are also shown; national forest road junctions are often signed with these numbers.

The U.S. Geological Survey series of 7.5-minute topographic maps is the most detailed available. Each map covers an area of about 7 miles by 9 miles at a scale of 1:24,000, or 1 inch to 2,000 feet. Computerized methods are used to produce these extremely accurate maps from aerial photography. The sheer number of maps makes it difficult to revise them very often, so trails, roads, and other manmade features may be shown incorrectly. Also, don't rely on springs and permanent streams shown on USGS maps unless you can confirm their presence with a ranger, another experienced outdoor person, or a guidebook.

Wilderness and recreation maps are often best. These show an entire wilderness or park on one map and are updated frequently. Land management agencies and private companies publish maps for certain popular desert wilderness and recreation areas. Local backcountry regulations and guidelines are often shown.

DESERT HIKING ESSENTIALS

Of all items needed for a safe desert adventure, survival and first-aid items are the most important; and the equipment for safe desert hiking differs somewhat from what is needed for trips in well-watered country. On the following page is a list of the items you should always carry, no matter the length of the trip. Remember the essentials. (Refer to Appendix B for a complete list of gear.)

DESERT HIKING ESSENTIALS
water
sun hat (brimmed hat)
sunglasses (good quality)
sunscreen
extra clothing
lighter (fire-starting material/matches)
pocketknife
flashlight or headlamp (extra batteries and bulbs)
compass
signal mirror
map
extra food
first-aid kit
repair kit
insect repellent
toilet paper

Water usually is the most important and heaviest item in your pack. Refer to page 14 for a thorough discussion of water gear and difficulties.

A **sun hat** with a brim that can keep your head cool is essential to avoiding heat-related health problems.

⸙

Sunglasses are essential in the intense desert light of spring and summer. Avoid cheap ones. Most are made of plastic and don't protect your eyes from damaging ultraviolet light. In fact, wearing poor-quality sunglasses can be worse than wearing no sunglasses at all. Your pupils open in response to the decreased visible light and admit more ultraviolet light than they would without sunglasses. The manufacturers of high-quality sunglasses not only make distortion-free lenses but also specify the amount of ultraviolet, infrared, and visible light transmitted.

⸙

Use **sunscreen** with a sun protection factor (SPF) of at least 15; SPF 30 or higher is better. The hot desert sun will burn your skin quickly, even if you already have a tan.

⸙

Bring an **extra layer of clothing,** such as a fleece jacket or a shell. You might be surprised to learn that cold can be a problem in the desert. After dark, temperatures fall rapidly, even in summer, because of the clear, dry air. The best seasons for desert hiking are fall, winter, and spring, and cold can be even more of a factor during these seasons.

⸙

Always carry some means of starting an emergency fire. Disposable **cigarette lighters** are light and provide a sustained flame. Stash at least two in your pack.

You can use a **pocketknife** to prepare kindling from wet desert wood in an emergency. If you have a deluxe model, you can use the scissors to cut moleskin, and use any other features for repairs and cooking chores.

Carry an **extra bulb** and **extra batteries** for your **flashlight or headlamp,** and know how long fresh batteries last. Always have a spare set of batteries (or several sets on long backpack trips).

Buy a quality **liquid-filled compass.** You don't necessarily need sighting mirrors and all the extra features for general desert travel, but these features may be useful. See page 46 for more information.

Get a **signal mirror** with a sighting grid, which makes the mirror more accurate and easier to use. Glass mirrors produce a far brighter flash than metal or plastic ones, but a small glass mirror can work just as well as a large one.

Remember your **map** and how to use it. See page 42 for more information.

Always store several extra **energy bars** (granola or snack bars) that won't melt in your emergency/survival kit. You may really appreciate that extra bar on a trip you pack short or in an emergency situation.

WATER

Desert hiking centers on the issue of water. A person doing strenuous hiking in hot weather may need as much as 2 gallons of water per day to avoid serious dehydration. In addition, water is heavy—8.3 pounds per gallon. The availability of water sources usually controls your trip itinerary. On day hikes, you can carry all the water you need, although it can still be quite a load in the hot summer.

WATER ESSENTIALS
filter system (see page 19)
iodine tablets (see page 20)
plastic water bottles (see page 16)
collapsible containers (see page 16)

When backpacking, carefully plan your trip so that you pass at least one reliable water source per day. **Water sources** include permanent or seasonal streams, springs, water pockets or tanks, and water caches placed in advance. It can be difficult to determine whether a water source is in fact reliable, but it's critical, especially in hot weather. Consult hikers experienced in the area, guidebooks, and the land management agencies for information. As you gain experience, you will be able to predict, based on recent weather, whether seasonal water sources will be available.

Don't rely on maps for water source information. Even the otherwise excellent U.S. Geological Survey topographic series maps often show springs that have long been dry and are notorious for showing permanent desert streams where, in reality, water flows only during wet weather.

Always have a backup plan in case a critical water source is dry. For example, you should make sure you have enough water to backtrack to the last source or to change your route to one with more water.

A **massive load of water** can slow you down enough to force a change in your trip plans. Keep this in mind when first planning your trip. During the trip, you may find less water than you expected, and have to carry more water than you planned. Bring along extra collapsible containers just in case.

Water is scarce; keep it clean. Keep human waste, soap, and food scraps out of drainages, whether or not they are dry at the moment. Never bathe or swim in a water pocket or tank. Even if you don't use soap, you'll still disturb the natural environment by stirring up sand and sediment. Some animals, such as the spadefoot toad, depend on the sediment for successful reproduction.

If water sources are small, **take only the water you need** for drinking and cooking. In addition, don't waste it. If water is scarce, even brushing your teeth should be avoided. Remember, you're the guest in the desert backcountry; don't depriv your hosts of water they need to survive.

⸙

Buy bottles made of **high-density polyethylene,** polycarbonate, polypropylene, or other plastics that do not flavo water.

⸙

Many extended desert backpack trips are only possible i you're willing to carry water for two or three days of dr hiking. Plastic bottles are very bulky, so consider **collapsible water containers.** These are available in sizes up t 2 gallons or more. The advantage is that empty container don't take up much room in your pack; the disadvantage i that they aren't as reliable as rigid containers.

⸙

My preference in collapsible containers is a **nylon water bag** The outer shell is made from nylon pack cloth and include a carrying handle. The inner shell or water bladder is doubl plastic with a built-in, removable spigot or spout. The nylon shell is slightly smaller than the bladder, so the shell take the weight of the water. I've dropped full bags several fee onto rock without damage. Their capacity is slightly ove 2 gallons, and if the bag is not quite filled, it can be efficiently squeezed into your pack. The bladder and spigot ca be replaced when they wear out, and the plastic doesn't flavor water. There are a couple of disadvantages. It's very eas to accidentally puncture the bladder with cactus spines and the like, so in camp, I try to hang the bag whenever possible. If I have to put it on the ground, I lay it on a clean rock or on a piece of my equipment. The other problem is that the spigot tends to leak if something in your pack presses up against it. To avoid that, I put the bag spigot side up in my pack, then place a drinking cup (which I carry anyway) over the spigot to protect it. It would be nice to see an improved version with a screw-on spigot. Despite these difficulties, the weight savings are definitely worth it.

In very hot weather, when your water supply is critical, it's a good idea to carry a **number of small containers,** rather than one or two large containers. Or, compromise and carry a couple of 1-quart bottles with enough collapsible containers to hold the maximum amount of water you'll need to carry on the trip.

Make sure your bottles have **reliable seals.** You should test them before the trip by turning filled bottles upside down and squeezing them hard. Test collapsible containers before a trip by blowing them up with air by mouth, then letting them sit for a while to see if they maintain pressure.

How much water should you carry? There are no rigid rules for the amount of water to carry. Some areas are well watered, and two 1-quart bottles of water should be enough.

In other areas, water sources may be two to three days apart; if the weather is cool (fall, winter, spring), a couple of gallons must be carried. In hot weather (summer), hiking for two to three days between water sources can be deadly and is not recommended.

On **day hikes,** I carry 1 to 4 quarts depending upon hike length, difficulty, heat, and water sources.

On **backpacking trips,** I usually carry two 1-quart bottles and a 2-gallon water bag for maximum flexibility and minimum weight or bulk. On extended trips, I carry a spare bladder.

If you'll be collecting water from **shallow rain pockets,** bring along a small bottle or shallow cup with a thin rim. Some people carry large plastic syringes for this purpose.

Duct tape will repair most water bottles and collapsible containers. You can repair a nylon water bag by turning the bag inside out through the spigot.

Keep your water containers inside your pack and insulated by clothing. Bottles carried on your belt or fanny pack quickly become warm and stale. Don't use metal canteens because they heat up rapidly.

FINDING EMERGENCY WATER
Look for **patches of lighter green vegetation** in drainages or on distant slopes, which can mark springs. Water pockets often form in dry washes where rock outcrops have trapped an earlier flow of water.
Plunge pools at the bases of dry falls may hold water.
Damp areas in otherwise dry streambeds are an indication that water is near the surface. Before you start to dig for it, check around the corner. Chances are the water will surface either upstream or downstream.
In basin and range country, streams may flow down out of the mountains and disappear into the ground abruptly when the stream crosses the fault line at the foot of the range. Large expanses of open, flat, or domed rock often harbor rain pockets. Sandstone country is especially good for rain pockets. Larger pockets will hold water for weeks after a storm.

Purify all water before use. Even sparkling clear water may contain dangerous organisms. There are several reliable methods for purifying water, including filtration, boiling, and iodine treatment.

Filters are popular because they preserve the taste of the water. They vary in effectiveness, so shop carefully. All **good filters remove disease-causing bacteria and cysts,** and are excellent for removing visible contaminants such as algae and tiny insects. Make sure you get a filter that uses an active iodine element to kill viruses. Filtering alone can't remove viruses, which are too small for the filter element to trap.

Filters have disadvantages. They are heavy and tend to clog up, especially in murky water. Make sure you know how to field-clean your filter before relying on it.

⁂

Desert water often contains bits of leaves and other organic material. A **lightweight filter system** can be made from paper coffee filters and a plastic filter holder. Don't try to use coffee filters alone—they work very slowly without the support of the holder. Iodine tablets, the optional iodine remover tablets (see discussion on page 21), coffee filters, and the filter holder make up a water purification system that can handle any desert water source and still weighs much less than a regular water filter.

⁂

Boiling is a reliable purification method. Boiling kills all viruses and disease-causing organisms at any altitude because the boiling point is always high enough to sterilize the water.

⁂

Boiling takes time and fuel, and the water tastes flat afterward. You can **improve the taste of boiled water** by pouring it back and forth between two containers several times, which aerates the water and helps it cool.

⁂

Iodine tablets are also very reliable for purifying water, if used correctly. Follow the directions on the bottle exactly and keep the tablets dry. You may also want to carry a second bottle in case one opens accidently in your pack.

Make iodine water taste better with the iodine remover tablets that come with some brands of iodine tablets. You can also use fruit or sport drink mixes to hide the taste. Both methods use ascorbic acid (vitamin C), which deactivates the iodine in the water. Be sure you've allowed enough time for the iodine to work before adding the remover tablets or drink mix to the water.

Avoid carrying water bottles outside your pack; the sun heats the water and rots plastic bottles.

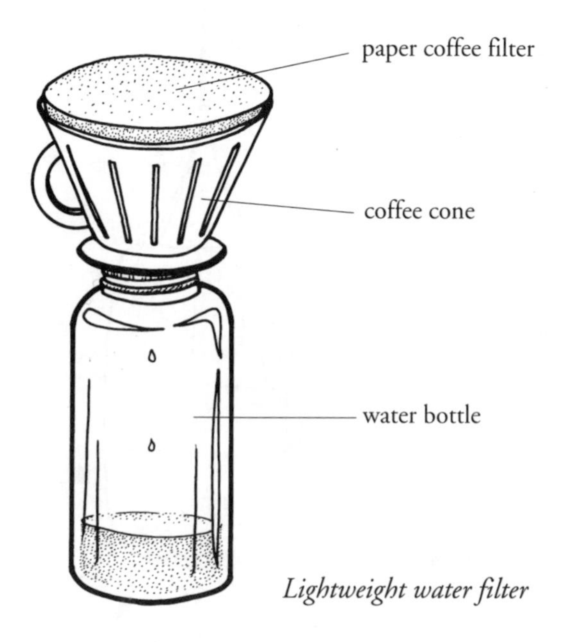

Lightweight water filter

If you don't have a filter but do have a nylon water bag, you can **get clear water** when the source is muddy or silty. Fill the water bag and add iodine tablets, then hang the bag so that the bottom corner opposite the spigot (spout) is the lowest point. Allow the water to settle for an hour or more. The silt and sediment will settle into the low corner, leaving the rest of the water relatively clear. Next, draw off water without disturbing the bag.

Water bag as sediment trap

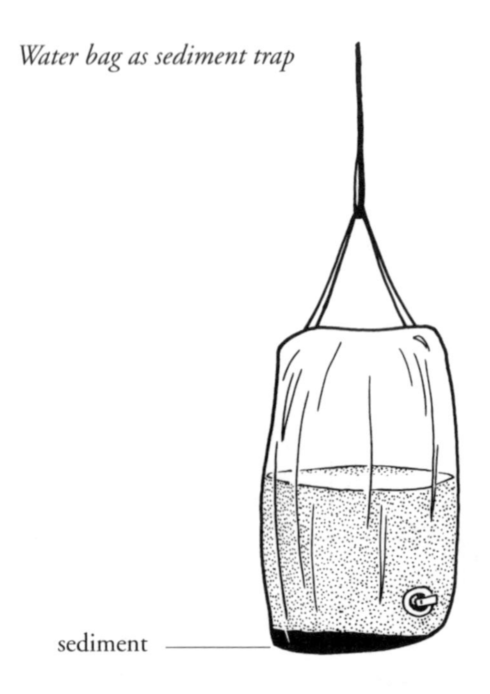

FOOTWEAR

After proper fit, **ventilation is the important feature** to look for in desert hiking boots. Waterproof boots are seldom necessary. Avoid heavy, full-grain leather boots. If you insist on waterproof boots, consider a model made with one of the lightweight waterproof/breathable fabrics such as Gore-Tex. Many of the recent lightweight designs work well in the desert.

⇜

Look for a **shoe with durable toe and heel caps,** as well as reinforced stitching, because desert trails tend to be rocky and abrasive.

⇜

Exploring canyons frequently requires wading or swimming. **Non-leather hiking boots** or shoes work better than leather, because the water collected while wading can escape during dry stretches. Also try sport sandals, which can double as relaxing camp shoes (except in the warm summer months, when snakes are active).

⇜

Heat and sweat buildup in your boots can cause **blisters.** The old hiker's trick of wearing two pairs of socks works well. The thick outer sock provides cushioning, and the thin liner sock clings to your skin and prevents the outer sock from rubbing and causing blisters. Wool is hard to beat for the outer sock, because it retains its loft better than synthetics or cotton when damp with sweat.

For the inner layer, polypropylene liner socks do an excellent job of wicking sweat away from your skin, but some people don't like the feel of the synthetic fiber against their skin. Thin **cotton liner socks** are a good compromise for the inner layer. Other hikers prefer a single cotton athletic sock, especially in hot weather.

If you're caught in **cold, wet weather** with nonwaterproof boots, wear a pair of plastic bags over your outer socks as a vapor barrier. Gallon-size freezer bags with zipper closures work well and double as resealable trash bags. Although some moisture will build up from perspiration, your feet will be warmer than they would be if your socks were completely soaked.

WALKING STICKS

A **walking stick** can be helpful, especially for rough slopes, stream crossings, or other places where the footing is uncertain. The stick can also be used to push brush and low branches out of the way, probe potential hiding areas during snake season, prop up a pack into a backrest, or support a tarp for shelter from the weather.

Attach a small **loop of nylon cord** to the top of your walking stick. The loop lets you hang the stick from your wrist when you need both hands for a moment. It also makes it easier to attach a tarp once you reach camp.

Using the walking stick loop

CLOTHING

Keep your skin covered with a long-sleeved shirt and long pants. Long pants will also protect your skin from scratches when hiking a brushy trail.

Shorts are comfortable, but if you wear them, use a good sunscreen. The intense desert sun can produce a painful sunburn in a short time, even on tanned skin.

Protect your head. In cold weather, up to half your body heat loss is through your head, because of all the blood vessels close to your skin. For the same reason, protect your head from summer sun with a good sun hat. Some hikers like floppy, broad-brimmed cotton hats; others like the "desert rat" style with a long flap in the back. Whatever the style, it should not only keep the sun out of your eyes but also shade your neck and ears. Baseball-style caps are only a little better than no hat at all.

The **four-layer system** is versatile enough to handle nearly any weather condition and helps keep your load light. The first, inner layer consists of lightweight, synthetic, moisture-wicking long underwear. A pair of sturdy pants (with shorts as a warm-weather option) and a sturdy long-sleeved shirt that will hold up to brush and rocks form the second layer. The third layer consists of an insulating jacket or parka. The fourth layer consists of a good pair of rain pants and jacket with hood or a waterproof and breathable outer layer.

THE FOUR-LAYER SYSTEM
1. Lightweight synthetic underwear
2. Long-sleeved shirt and long pants or shorts
3. Down or pile jacket
4. Rain pants and jacket

In dry weather, down is the lightest, most durable, and **most practical insulation** in the desert. However, when wet, down loses insulating value and does not dry quickly. Consider a jacket insulated with a synthetic fill (pile) if you expect wet weather. Synthetic fleece is the warmest, driest insulator for wet conditions. Even after getting completely soaked, you can wring out synthetic fleece and wear it immediately. Check the forecast before you go, then you can decide whether to take pile or down.

Don't put up with being **overheated or chilled.** While hiking, stop to add or subtract layers as necessary to stay comfortable. Add layers until you feel warm in cool weather, and seek shade until you feel cool in hot weather. Drinking extra water can also help you cool down.

FOOD

One desert-hiking myth is that since you have to carry water anyway, why not save a step and carry hydrated food? This means either fresh food, which doesn't keep, or canned food, which is heavy and leaves you carrying the empty cans for the entire trip. Moreover, many desert hikes have enough springs and other water sources so that you don't have to carry a huge load of water all the time. A great deal of specialty dehydrated food is made for backpacking and lightweight camping, but it is very expensive. Many items found in supermarkets make good backpacking food at a lower cost. Using just supermarket food, I have been able to do many backpack trips with no more than 1 pound 10 ounces of food per person per day.

DESERT MENU
Breakfast: low-bulk cold cereals with powdered milk, hot cereals, dried fruit, breakfast bars, hot chocolate, tea, and coffee bags.
Lunch: munchies such as nuts, hard cheese, crackers, dried fruit, candy bars (not chocolate), athletic energy bars, dried soup, hard candy, beef or turkey jerky, sardines, and fruit-flavored drink mixes.
Dinner: dried noodle or rice-based dishes possibly supplemented with a small can of tuna, turkey, or chicken.

Of course, on a day hike you can carry **fresh fruit,** fresh food for sandwiches, or anything else. A juicy, sweet orange is a real delight on a hot summer hike!

Always keep an **energy bar** or two in your pack so that you always have something to eat even if you forget to bring lunch.

Avoid chocolate, which melts easily, and perishable foods such as soft cheeses and butter.

On multiday trips when you have to carry water for dry camps, plan to use **minimum water foods.** These include noodle or rice meals that use only enough water to hydrate the food, with no extra to pour off, and are easy to clean up.

Macaroni is not a minimum water food, because it requires extra water for cooking and straining noodles.

⇜

On warmer trips or when you'll have to carry a lot of water, **consider leaving your stove behind** and eating trail munchies and other food that doesn't require cooking. (Remember to always carry emergency fire-starting material.)

⇜

Before leaving home, **remove excess packaging** such as cardboard boxes. Plastic bags with zipper closures (zip-locked bags) make excellent food repackaging bags. Double-bag messy items. If you do bring along margarine and peanut butter, pack them in reliable wide-mouth plastic jars (available from outdoor suppliers). Put the container in a plastic bag, too.

⇜

Extra **zipper-locked bags** are also useful during the trip for double-bagging messy trash such as sardine or tuna cans. Zipper-locked bags make good trash bags because the airtight seal minimizes food odors that attract wildlife.

⇜

Dedicate one or more **nylon stuff sacks** to food storage and don't use them for anything else during the trip. The idea is to confine food odors as much as possible to avoid attracting rodents and other animals. Bears are not usually a problem, but rodents can wreak havoc on your food supply.

Use your pack as a cooler. When loading your pack in the morning, place food bags deep within your backpack and insulate them with a down or pile jacket. Try to keep your pack in the shade during rest stops. The temperature in the shade may be 5–15 degrees cooler than in the strong desert sun.

STOVES

If you use a **butane stove,** don't count on buying more fuel canisters in a remote desert region. Take all you'll need from home.

It's common for stoves to clog with sand and dust on desert trips. Make sure you have a stove repair kit that includes a **jet cleaner.** Some stoves have built-in jet cleaning mechanisms; these can save a lot of time and frustration.

Use a **windscreen.** In the desert, strong winds often blow for hours at a time, especially in the spring. Even a slight breeze greatly reduces the efficiency of an unprotected stove, which means you'll use a lot more fuel, and cooking takes longer.

Component stoves, in which the burner and fuel tank assemblies are separate, often have windscreens that completely enclose the burner. This design works very well and protects the flame even in strong winds. It also increases the efficiency of the stove in calm air.

Conventional stoves, designed with the burner and fuel tank as a single unit, are generally more convenient because they do not have to be assembled before use. The windscreen never encloses the burner completely, because doing so would allow too much heat to reach the fuel tank. To protect the stove from wind, you'll have to build a windbreak using your pack, other gear, or stones. **Warning:** Never use any type of windscreen to enclose both the burner and fuel tank on any stove. The fuel tank can easily overheat and explode. During use, periodically check the temperature of the fuel tank. If the tank gets more than warm to the touch, turn the stove off.

BACKPACKS

Many experienced desert hikers still use **external frame packs** because of their superior air circulation. In fairness, some internal frame packs provide good airflow around your back. Of course, internal frame packs provide better balance for rough, cross-country desert walking.

Desert day hikers often prefer **fanny packs** for the same reason. The major drawback is that sometimes you can't carry enough water in a small pack.

Since **water is the heaviest** item in your pack, keep it close to your back for better balance. Don't put large amounts of water at the bottom or top of your pack.

TENTS AND TARPS

Many desert backpackers prefer to **sleep under the stars** when they can. In the dry, clear desert air, the horizon-to-horizon blaze of stars is an unforgettable sight. Still, deserts do have periods of rainy, snowy, or cold and windy weather, making shelter necessary.

Sleeping on the ground is not advisable during the warmer months. In hot weather, most desert creatures, including snakes and insects, are nocturnal, and a floored and completely zippered tent is comforting. As for use anywhere, sound construction and high quality is important. However, a heavy four-season tent is overkill in the desert.

A net tent, in which all or part of the canopy is fine no-see-um netting, is often the ideal desert shelter. A conventional waterproof fly covers the net canopy in the event of bad weather but can be left off (but not left behind!) during most desert nights.

Net tent without fly

Avoid the weight and expense of a tent by carrying a nylon tarp with a separate groundsheet. A tarp provides good weather protection if set up properly and is versatile enough to use as a sunshade or windbreak during lunch stops. Remember that a tarp provides no protection from mosquitoes and other insects. Using a tarp effectively does take some practice. Consider that you may have no trees with which to set up your tarp.

A **walking stick** can double as a tarp pole. Alternatively, you may be able to use large boulders as supports.

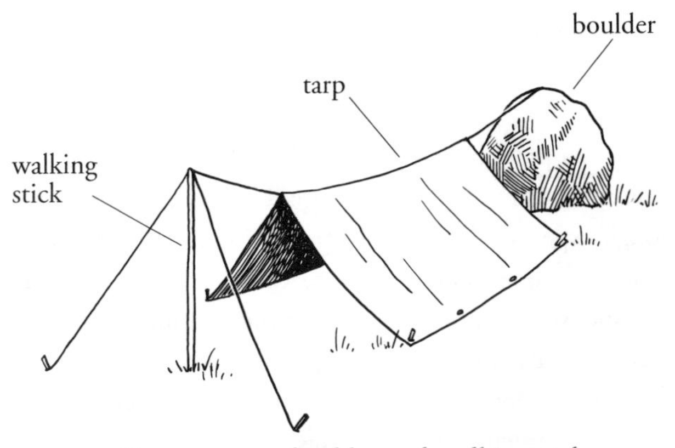

Tarp set up on boulder and walking stick

Another tent alternative, especially for solo hikers, is the **bivouac sack,** an outer layer of waterproof and breathable fabric that covers your sleeping bag and head. Designs range from simple sleeping bag covers with a bit of netting over the opening to one-person tents. Their weights are similar to that of tarps. Bivy sacks are more secure in bad weather than tarps but not nearly as spacious.

The midday **desert sun quickly rots nylon tents** and tarps. If you have to leave your shelter up all day, try to place it in the shade. Otherwise, take it down for the day and put it back up in the evening. The low-angle sun at morning and evening will do little damage to nylon.

SLEEPING BAGS

A **three-season bag** (+10 degrees F) is good for most desert hiking. In summer, you can save weight by carrying a lighter bag.

Down is a practical insulator for desert sleeping bags, because sustained wet weather is rare. High-quality down fill, though expensive, is still unsurpassed in insulating capability for its weight. Since it is more durable, down is actually less expensive than synthetics over the lifetime of the bag. **Synthetic fills** have the advantages of lower initial cost and of retaining most of their insulating ability when soaking wet. I recommend synthetic bags for trips during the **wet season** (winter to early spring) when it may be difficult to stay dry. Otherwise, I prefer down.

SLEEPING PADS

The best type of sleeping pad is a **self-inflating foam-filled air mattress.** These are less prone to puncture, warmer, and at least as comfortable as traditional air mattresses. Regular foam pads are a cheap alternative. They insulate very well and don't puncture, but are not as comfortable as self-inflating models.

Check for spines and thorns before laying out your mattress, and always use a ground sheet or a tent floor under it.

Check for leaks in your self-inflating mattress before a trip. Squeeze all of the air out by rolling it up as tightly as possible, close the valve securely, and let it sit overnight. If it unrolls, air leaked in, which means it has pinhole leaks.

The hardest part of **repairing tiny cactus spine punctures** in a self-inflating mattress (the kind of holes that take half the night to let you down) is finding them. Blow up the pad as hard as you can, then sit on it in still water or in a bathtub. Look for tiny streams of bubbles, and mark all the leaks with a pencil. Dry the pad, and then repair the holes with the cement recommended by the manufacturer. I find that a good, flexible contact cement also works well. This tip is best for home, but I have done it in the field!

VEHICLE PREPARATION

Consider traveling with more than one vehicle in case one breaks down. Approaches do not always require two vehicles, but there is a significant difference between a maintained five-mile approach road driven in cool weather and a hundred-mile unmaintained road driven in hot weather. A vehicle breakdown on the former is inconvenient; on the latter, deadly.

Keep your vehicle reliable by **practicing preventive maintenance.** Fifty miles from the nearest service station is no place to have an old fan belt break. Before leaving home, check coolant, oil levels, and tire pressure and overall condition. Don't forget to check your spare tire. Some desert drivers carry a can or two of tire repair/inflator. It can save the day if you experience a puncture.

Keep a set of **basic tools,** including a sturdy shovel, in your car and learn how to use them. In sandy areas, consider carrying sand mats made from old pieces of carpet.

VEHICLE SUPPLIES
spare tire
a few cans of emergency tire inflator
lug wrench
jack
jumper cables
extra oil
extra drinking/radiator water
extra food
change of clothes for return
sand mats
shovel
tow chain
spare parts as appropriate

Carry a tow chain or cable. Sometimes another car comes by, but don't depend on the driver to have a tow chain. I prefer to carry an old climbing rope or a length of climber's nylon webbing, because they're easier to attach and more versatile.

Carry extra water and food in your car in case you are stuck or stranded. Think in terms of being able to survive for several days, until searchers find you.

When leaving the last outpost of civilization for desert back roads, fill up your **fuel tank.** Driving on sandy or rocky roads and using four-wheel drive uses more fuel than highway or city driving.

DRIVING DESERT ROADS

Review the approach ahead of time. In some desert areas, new roads are commonly made by vehicles driving cross-country. Also, consider that road signs may be missing.

Road maintenance is infrequent on desert dirt roads. Washouts, potholes, deep sand, ruts, and other obstacles can appear suddenly, so watch your speed on otherwise smooth, maintained roads.

Deep sand is a hazard on some approach roads; a **four-wheel-drive** vehicle may be necessary.

Low-clearance vehicles should stick to well-maintained roads. Check your guidebook and ask land managers before relying on a car meant for the highway.

Stay on the established roadway, whether it's a maintained road or a jeep trail. Vehicle tracks easily scar desert land; the evidence from irresponsible off-highway vehicle use, four-wheeling, and desert-vehicle racing will be visible for many years.

Respect all **road closures** and signs.

⇜

If you have to **turn around** on a desert road, remember that the shoulders may be very soft. Turn around by remaining on the traveled or maintained surface.

⇜

If you're in doubt about a bad section of road, especially if there's a dropoff, check it out on foot. Don't hesitate to do a little rock moving and roadwork if needed. **Driving slowly** also allows you to stop and, most of the time, back out if you start to lose traction.

⇜

If you become stuck and can't move with **gentle application of power,** stop. Don't try to power out—you'll just power yourself into a pit.

GETTING "UN-STUCK"
1. If you have four-wheel drive and get stuck while in two-wheel drive, shift into four-wheel drive and gently try to move out.
2. If that fails, get out and survey the situation.
3. If you're traveling with another vehicle, the quickest way to get out is to have them tow you. If that's not practical, or if yours is the only vehicle, then you'll have a bit more work to do.
4. If the wheels sink into soft sand but the vehicle is not high centered, you may be able to get out by digging the sand away from the tires so you can move with little power. Sand mats will help maintain traction (see illustration below). Rubber floor mats can also be used for this purpose. If you're high-centered, then jack up the wheels one at a time, fill in the hole, and lay down your sand mats or other firm material (small tree or bush branches work well) under the tire and to the rear. Once all is ready, carefully ease back onto firm ground.

Using sand mats

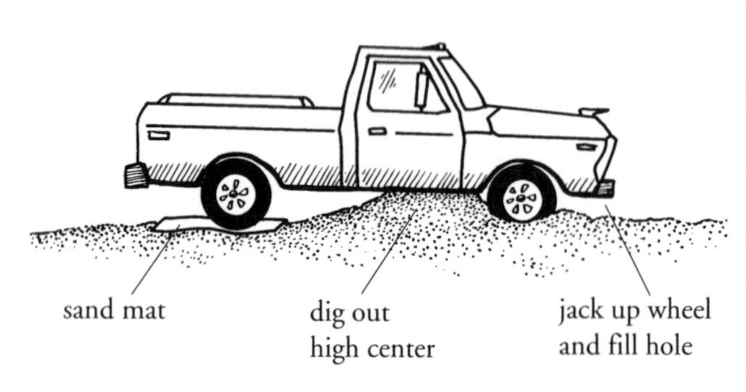

Don't cross flooded washes. The roadbed may be eroded away and the water is probably much deeper and swifter than it appears.

❧

Don't park in a dry wash or streambed, especially during the late summer thunderstorm season. A distant storm may cause the wash to flash flood without warning.

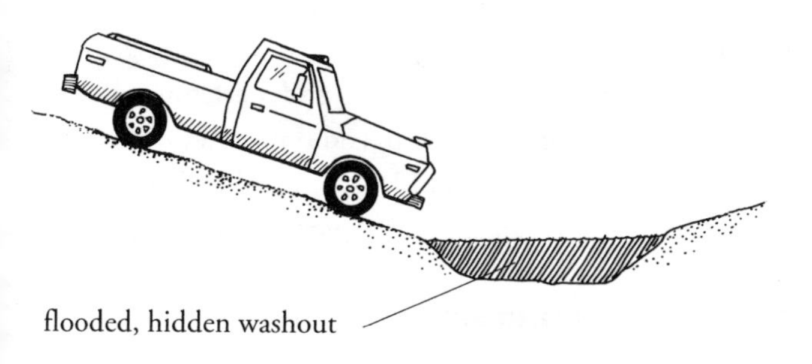

Flooded, washed-out road

Consider that **washes crossed** on the way to the trailhead might be flooding and impassable on the way out.

Flooding from summer thunderstorms usually subsides in a few hours. On the other hand, flooding can be prolonged for days if caused by heavy winter or spring rain, especially if melting snow in the high country adds to the runoff.

In some desert areas, **severe sandstorms** can occur that may suddenly reduce visibility to zero. These are more of a hazard on freeways and highways than on back roads. If you encounter suddenly reduced visibility, drive completely clear of the roadway, and turn off all lights. Many accidents occur when panicked drivers stop suddenly in the traffic lane. If you leave your lights on, even if you're clear of the road, other drivers may see your lights and steer toward them, thinking you're on the road. In addition, wind-driven sand can seriously damage windshield glass and body paint. You can minimize this damage by stopping until the wind abates.

USING MAP AND COMPASS

Desert hiking usually involves **faint trails and cross-country travel.** Map-reading skills are essential.

The best way to **learn to read topographic maps** is to buy one for an area you already know. By comparing the features of the terrain with its depiction on the map, you'll quickly master the art of map reading.

Contour lines are the essential feature of topographic maps. Each line represents a constant elevation above sea level.

Where the terrain is gentle, the lines are spread apart. Closely spaced contour lines mean that the terrain is steep. Ridges and drainages are shown by U- or V-shaped lines. Thin blue lines representing an intermittent or permanent stream usually distinguish drainages.

If contour lines are missing, there's a vertical or overhanging cliff. It's especially important to note missing contours along narrow canyon bottoms, which usually means there's one or more pour offs or dry waterfalls. You may or may not be able to find a route down or around these obstacles.

Missing contour lines

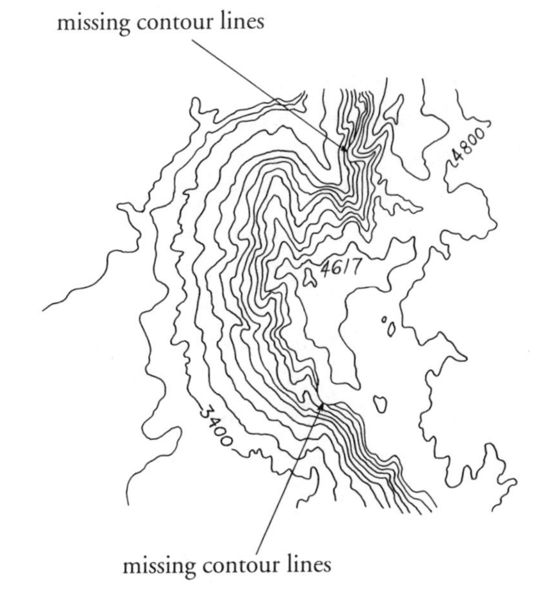

Learn the symbols used on your topographic map. Wilderness and recreation area maps usually have a legend printed on the map. The U.S. Geological Survey will provide a free legend for their topographic maps on request.

❧

Don't rely on **permanent streams** shown on maps of desert country. They may not be reliable sources of water. Often maps show seasonal water that just happened to be present during surveying. The same is true of springs.

❧

Learn the difference between **true north,** as shown on maps, and **magnetic north,** the direction your compass needle points. True north is the direction to the Earth's geographic North Pole. Compass needles align themselves with the earth's magnetic field, and generally point toward a spot in northeastern Canada about a thousand miles from the geographic pole. **Declination** (also called variation) is the difference between true and magnetic north. Because the magnetic field changes slowly, declination in a given location changes with time. Good maps show the declination as of publication date, and may show the rate of change. Declination can be as much as 20 degrees in the western U.S., which will cause large errors if you don't correct for it. (There's yet a third "north," **grid north,** which is the difference between the grid lines on the map and true north. For most fieldwork, you can ignore it. It's usually only a fraction of a degree.)

To help you relate the map to **the landscape around you,** orient the map and yourself toward true north. All good maps are printed with north toward the top of the sheet as a standard. Use your compass to determine north. Locate visible terrain features on the map, keeping in mind that desert objects are often much farther away than they appear. After you become familiar with the country, you'll be able to relate the map to terrain features without orienting it.

Triangulation can be used to identify unknown landmarks, such as mountain peaks, but you must be sure of your own current position. Take a compass bearing on the landmark, and then plot the bearing on your map, starting from your position. Use a protractor or the baseplate of your compass. Remember that you're working with magnetic bearings *to* the landmarks. The line will run through the unknown landmark. If the bearing line crosses several possible landmarks, hike a bit further and take another bearing. The two map lines will intersect at the landmark.

Resection (often incorrectly called triangulation) can be used if you are unsure of your position, but have one or more known landmarks in sight. Take a bearing on each of the landmarks. If you have a single landmark to work with, you'll at least know that your position is along the bearing line. If you also know that you're on a linear feature, such as a trail, road, ridge, or drainage, then the point where the bearing line crosses that feature on your map is your position. With two or more bearings, your position is shown by the intersection of the bearings on your map.

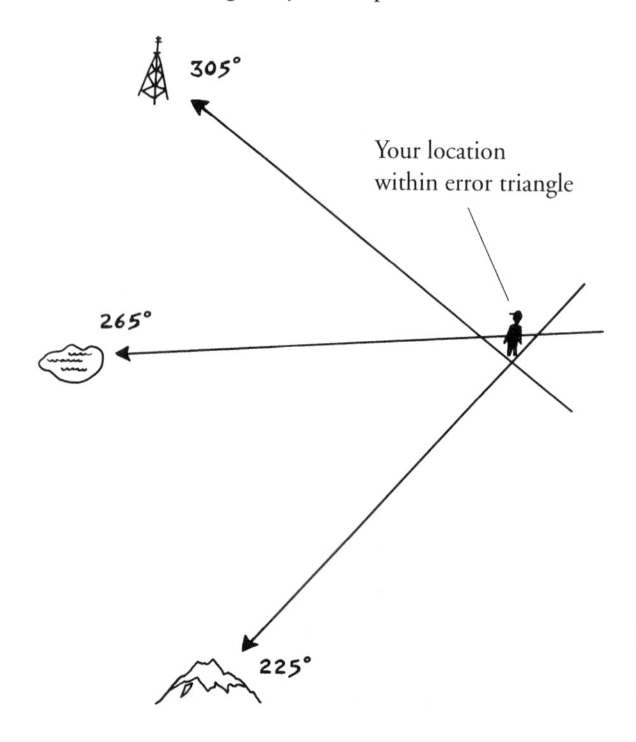

Resection with map and compass

A **compass with a sighting mirror** is more accurate, and an adjustable declination setting lets you work with true bearings without having to correct for magnetic variation.

The type of compass with a clear plastic baseplate and a rotating bearing ring works well for plotting bearing lines on a map. Use the straight edge of another map to extend the compass straight edge if necessary.

USING GPS

A **Global Positioning System** receiver (GPS) is a hand-held device that uses satellites to determine the exact coordinates of your location. It can make desert route-finding easier, especially on unmarked roads that cross open desert valleys or plateaus with few landmarks. Because it is unaffected by weather or darkness, GPS can help you navigate when landmarks are poor or not visible.

When planning a hike where you know **finding the trailhead** or departure point will be difficult, use the map to determine the coordinates of the trailhead. Enter these coordinates in your GPS unit ahead of time. Then, as you drive the back roads, the GPS receiver can help you determine which way to turn to keep heading toward the trailhead.

It may also be useful to enter the **coordinates of your turnoff** from the highway or major road if you suspect that it's unmarked. That can save a lot of time hunting up and down the highway for an obscure turnoff.

If your vehicle is not at an **actual trailhead** or other well-defined point, it might be hard to find on your return. Use the GPS to record the position before leaving on your hike. This technique is especially time saving when you have to park several miles out in a desert valley and hike to the foot of the mountains. The lower slopes (known as a *bajada*) are often laced with numerous parallel washes and low ridges that all look the same. It also helps to park on a ridge rather than in a low spot, so that you can see your vehicle from a distance.

Don't try to use a **GPS receiver** while on the move; the readout is inaccurate at walking speed. Instead, turn it on at rest stops to get an update on your progress and the direction to your goal.

Don't count on a GPS receiver for **canyon bottom navigation,** because often there aren't enough satellites in view for the unit to get a fix.

PACING AND WALKING STRATEGIES

In hot summer weather, consider adopting the **siesta system**: Start hiking at first light, then stop for a long break at around ten A.M., or whenever the heat becomes too much. Rest in the shade, have a leisurely lunch, then start hiking again when the blast furnace abates. This can be as late as five P.M. in very hot weather. You can get in seven or eight hours of hiking during long summer days while avoiding the worst of the heat.

Before leaving your vehicle, whether you'll be hiking on trail or cross-country, look at your map and **pick a baseline**.

A baseline is a road that borders one side of the area, a canyon rim, or any other feature that would be impossible to miss. Then, if you become completely disoriented, you can hike in the general direction of your baseline with the assurance that you will eventually reach it. Of course, hiking to your baseline is a last resort because it may take you many miles out of your way. Having a known baseline will make you more confident in your explorations.

Baselines

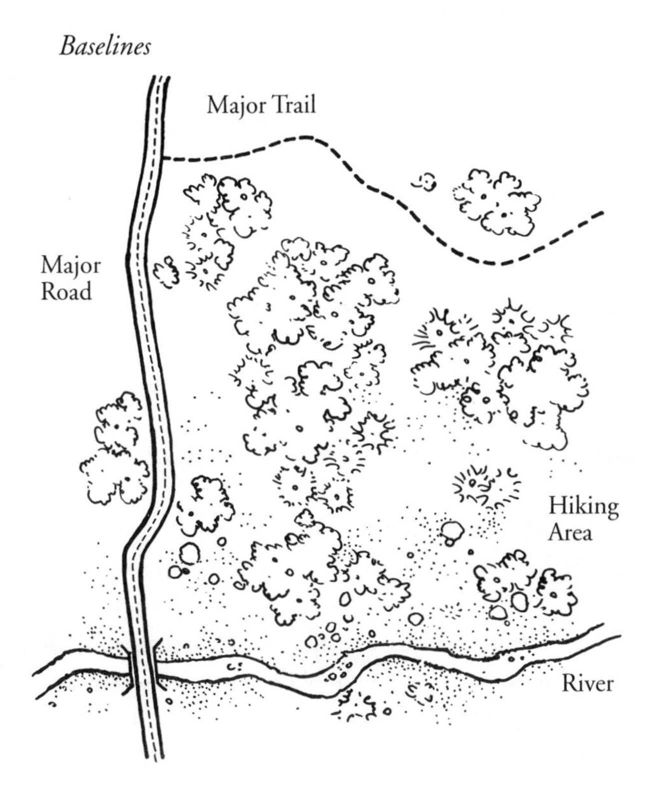

As you hike, **stay oriented** by paying attention to your direction of travel in relation to the position of the sun, wind direction, and slope of the ground and other terrain features.

⇜

If the **group plans to split up,** there should be an experienced desert hiker in each group. Agree on a meeting place and time, allowing extra time for delays, and make every effort to be there on time.

TRAIL HIKING

When trying to stay on a **faint trail,** note how the trail deals with streambed crossings and side canyons. Once you begin to see the pattern, you'll be able to pick out the trail on the opposite side before crossing.

⇜

Trail signs are often missing in remote desert areas where there is little trail maintenance. Refer to your map often, and remain aware of your position and direction of travel.

⇜

Rock cairns sometimes mark trails and routes in areas without trees. Trail crews usually build large, solid cairns. Treat smaller cairns with a healthy dose of skepticism—the person who built the cairn may have been off route.

⇜

When following a cairned trail or route, always **spot the next cairn** before leaving sight of the last. If necessary, walk expanding circles around the last cairn to find the next.

OFF-TRAIL HIKING

Cross-country hiking demands knowledge of the character of the landscape you're hiking. For example, ridges are usually the best routes of travel because brush chokes drainages. The best way to gain this type of knowledge is through experience in the area.

⋞

Many desert wildernesses have **no trails at all.** In this case, hike some of the trails in a similar area before graduating to trackless areas.

⋞

Game trails, especially those made by wild burros and horses, can make travel a lot easier if the trail goes in the direction you want to travel.

⋞

Obstacles such as steep, rocky slopes or cliffs, areas of heavy brush, and deep canyons usually make it impossible to follow a straight line. In desert canyon or mountain country, the classic orienteering technique of following a compass bearing (or a GPS course) directly to your destination rarely works.

⋞

Pick a distant, **unmistakable landmark** near your destination. Then, as you deviate around obstacles, use the landmark to maintain your general direction of travel. A GPS receiver can be used the same way.

As you hike, look back often to keep track of **your return route.** Landmarks change shape and appearance as you move and as the lighting changes during the day.

A small pair of **binoculars or a monocular** can be very useful for route-finding, because they allow you to check out terrain from a distance before you're committed to a route.

CANYON HIKING

Some deserts feature deep, **narrow canyons.** At least staying on the route is simple, especially if you're hiking downstream. However, it can be very difficult to determine how far you've progressed. One way to do this is to keep your map handy and use it to keep track of each twist and turn as you hike.

Narrow canyons may **flash flood** without warning. Numerous hikers have lost their lives in flooded canyons. Always check the weather forecast carefully before entering a narrow canyon.

When you're planning a canyon hike, note distinct side canyons or other landmarks on the map. As you hike, watch for these predetermined landmarks and note the time on the map as you reach each one. Then, **calculate your rate of travel** by dividing distance by time.

Use an **accurate altimeter** along with a large-scale topographic map to track your progress in very narrow canyons.

The altimeter should be temperature-compensated and read in 20-foot increments to match the accuracy of the map. Don't rely on cheap altimeters that read in 100-foot increments.

Many canyons require **technical climbing skills.** Smaller canyons and side canyons are often choked with obstacles. These include pools of standing water that may be too deep or cold to wade. Chockstones, large boulders that have fallen from above, often partially block narrow canyons, forming pouroffs—dry waterfalls that may be impossible to bypass without technical climbing gear.

A **lightweight air mattress** is a good way to float your pack across pools. If the water is too cold to wade or swim, you can use a small two-person pack raft.

LOST AND FOUND

It is important to **stay oriented** to your surroundings at all times. If a predicted landmark doesn't appear when you expected it, check your map before you get lost.

Don't hesitate to ask another hiker for directions, even in heavily used areas. The moment you become unsure of your position, *stop*. Take a rest break, have some water and food, and make a conscious effort to relax. Panic causes people to become seriously lost; continuing blindly on only makes the situation worse.

Evaluate your situation. If on a day hike, is it close to sunset? If so, do you have extra clothing, food, and water? If on a backpack trip, can you camp where you are? Does bad weather threaten? Is there a group member who's exhausted or has an injury or a medical problem? Take care of the most important things one at a time.

⇷

Use your stopping point as a **base to search for the route.** If you're following a faint trail or cairned route, look around for signs of the trail or the next cairn. The trail may have taken an unexpected sharp turn. If you can't locate the trail, then, if possible, backtrack to your **last known point**—a cairn, section of trail that's distinct, or a tree blaze.

⇷

Climb to a nearby hill or ridge and look for familiar landmarks. Look for **unique landmarks,** and use those to locate yourself on your map.

⇷

As a last resort, walk to your **predetermined baseline.** If you chose a good baseline, you'll eventually arrive at it, though at the cost of being hours or days late. Carefully consider the terrain you'll have to traverse to reach your baseline.

⇷

Should I walk downstream? The classic advice to follow a drainage river downstream to civilization may not always work in desert wilderness. In certain places, roads are built along ridgelines above canyon wilderness areas, and the best tactic is to follow ridges uphill. For example, the Canyonlands country of southeastern Utah is broken by narrow canyons that are often extremely deep and impossible to enter without technical climbing gear. In the central mountains of Arizona, dry waterfalls and deep pools often block canyon bottoms. These obstacles make travel rough and slow, or even impossible without special equipment. In such areas, ridges usually offer the easiest traveling. In the desert ranges of Nevada, southeastern California, and western Arizona, traveling downhill will take you to a highway or well-traveled dirt road, but you will be descending into hotter, drier country. Be sure you have enough water and endurance before attempting such a walk. When in doubt, stay put.

EMERGENCY SIGNALS

If you're completely disoriented, or an injury prevents you from traveling, then **stay put and signal.** If you let someone responsible know your plans before the trip, then searchers will eventually find you. You can help them find you more quickly by signaling. In North America, three of anything is the universal distress signal. You can use three fires, smoke columns, light flashes, or blasts on a whistle.

If you have a **signal mirror,** use it even if you haven't spotted a search vehicle or aircraft. In the desert, a mirror flash can be seen for 50 miles or more on a sunny day. Flash (by tapping or shaking the mirror) at any aircraft you spot, and regularly sweep the horizon with the mirror. Even if no one is searching for you, you'll eventually attract attention.

MINE HAZARDS

Desert areas have always been attractive to miners and prospectors because of the expanses of bare, often mineralized rock. Abandoned prospect holes and mineshafts are common. While land managers and mining authorities are making an attempt to secure dangerous sites, the sheer vastness of the problem leaves a lot of hazards in the desert backcountry. **Never enter any mineshaft.** Besides the obvious hazards of falling and the potential for collapse, old mines often contain poisonous or radioactive gasses, as well as unstable explosives and dangerous equipment. Report any explosives or other unusual hazards to the land management agency after your trip.

The presence of an **old road** may be a sign that there are old mines in the area.

When hiking **through heavy brush or at night,** be especially alert for old mineshafts. In areas that attracted a lot of prospecting, miners often dug numerous small pits. Even though these pits are usually only a few feet deep, coming upon one unaware can result in ankle or leg injuries or worse.

In mined areas, **stay away from the edges of vertical shafts,** even if covered. The edges of shafts often continue to crumble for years after abandonment. Also, avoid depressions in the ground—these may mark shafts or pits that have been covered with wood or metal that is rotting or rusting away.

WILDLIFE HAZARDS

Remember that **you're a visitor** when in wild desert country. Although humans have the responsibility to be careful stewards of the remaining wild lands and their animal and plant inhabitants, we are guests and should behave appropriately and respectfully. Most hazardous encounters with wild animals are a direct result of the human failing to act responsibly.

Never approach or **attempt to handle any wild animal.** All animals will defend themselves if they feel threatened or cornered. Even rabbits will bite to protect their young. By approaching or harassing wildlife, you are placing great stress on the animal and endangering yourself.

Mountain lions

Mountain lions or cougars are rare and elusive creatures in the remote country where they still survive. You'll be lucky to see tracks, let alone the animal. Most attacks happen after humans arouse the lion's predatory instincts by appearing to be prey. Running and mountain biking in lion country seems to have a slight chance of evoking the same response that a running deer causes.

If you do encounter a mountain lion, avoid prey-like reactions. Don't turn your back on the animal, and don't run. Make yourself appear as big and threatening as possible, and make unnatural sounds by rattling metal pots or the like. Mountain lion encounters usually result in just a fleeting glimpse of this magnificent animal. See *Mountain Lion Alert* (Falcon, 1997) for more information on dealing with mountain lion encounters.

Wolves and coyotes

Wolves have recently been reintroduced in some desert regions. They are not a hazard to humans. Neither are coyotes. The thrilling nocturnal howl of coyotes is as much a part of the desert as the clear, starry nights. We can only hope that the wolves are successful in their former ranges and that we will be lucky enough to hear their song as well.

Domestic cattle

Grazing occurs on much of the desert, so you may encounter cattle. Generally, cattle are used to humans and either avoid you or move away. It's possible that a bull could be dangerous, so it's a good idea to give cattle a reasonable margin as you pass them.

If you find the presence of cattle offensive in the backcountry, check with the land management agency before your trip. Cattle graze different areas at various times, and the rangers can tell you which areas to avoid.

In addition, you can avoid cattle by hiking in national parks, which don't allow grazing except in isolated cases.

Snakes and other reptiles

Desert rattlesnakes are fascinating animals, well adapted for life in the harsh environment. Rattlesnakes do not attack people, though they may accidentally crawl in your direction if they're not aware of your presence. Rattlesnakes are more sensitive to ground vibrations than to sound and ordinarily move quietly away from an approaching large animal such as a hiker. If surprised, they usually coil into a defensive posture and back slowly away. The snake creates its unmistakable buzzing rattle by shaking its tail so fast it blurs. When you hear the rattle, stop immediately and spot the snake before moving carefully away. Never handle or tease any snake. Bites usually occur on the feet or ankles. Ankle-high hiking boots and loose-fitting long pants can stop or reduce the severity of bites. Collectors suffer the vast majority of rattlesnake bites. It's very rare for a hiker to be bitten.

Rattlesnake bites can be distinguished from nonpoisonous snakebites by the two puncture wounds left by the venomous fangs, in addition to the regular tooth marks.

Develop the desert habit of **watching only the ground** in front of you while moving. Stop before looking around or at distant objects. This habit will save you from encounters with cactus and stepping into rodent burrows, as well as lessen your chance of a surprise confrontation with a rattlesnake.

Snakes prefer surfaces at about **80 degrees F**, so during hot weather they prefer the shade of bushes or rock overhangs, and in cool weather will be found sunning themselves on open ground. During cold weather, they are inactive. Any time lizards are active, rattlesnakes probably are active as well.

Since rattlesnakes can strike no further than about half their body length, avoid placing your hands and feet in areas you cannot see, and walk several feet away from **rock overhangs and shady ledges.**

Use a flashlight when moving around camp at dark, at least in the warmer months when snakes are active mainly at night. Never walk around camp barefoot or in sandals during the warm summer months.

Never kill rattlesnakes found in the wild. They are a vital part of the desert ecology and deserve respect. Do not handle a dead rattlesnake; they can strike by reflex for some time after apparent death.

You should carry a **snakebite kit** when snakes are active. Current medical opinion seems to agree that infection is as great a hazard as the venom. The amount of venom injected can vary greatly, and many bites, especially the common warning bites, inflict no venom at all. A good snakebite kit containing a suction syringe and antiseptic can be used to remove some venom immediately after the bite and to disinfect the wound site. Follow the instructions included with the kit, then get the victim to a hospital as soon as possible. Do not try the old practice of using a tourniquet or restricting band. This is now considered more dangerous than the bite itself.

The **Sonoran coral snake** is found only in the deserts of southern Arizona and northwestern Mexico. While extremely poisonous, it is reclusive, very small, and would have difficulty biting a human. All other desert snakes are nonpoisonous, though they may bite if handled.

A large lizard, the **Gila monster,** possesses venom similar to that of rattlesnakes but clamps on to its victim and grinds the venom into the wound with its molars. A rare and elusive reptile about a foot long that is protected by state law, the Gila monster is likely to bite only if handled or disturbed. Don't let its torpid appearance fool you—it can move very fast. Consider yourself very lucky if you even see one.

Insects

Poisonous insects are actually a greater hazard than rattlesnakes. The small, straw-colored **desert scorpion** likes to lurk under rocks and logs, and can give a sting that is life threatening to children. **Black widow spiders,** identifiable by the red hourglass-shaped mark on the underside, can inflict a dangerous bite. The **brown spider** inflicts a bite that may cause extensive tissue damage at the site, but is not generally life threatening. These bites seem minor at first but may become very painful after several hours. There is no specific field treatment; transport young children to a hospital as soon as possible. The dangerous-looking **centipede** can produce a painful bite and irritate skin with its sharp, clawed feet, but is not life threatening.

Avoid scorpions, spiders, and centipedes by not placing your hands and feet where you cannot see. Kick over rocks or logs before moving them with your hands. Don't unpack your sleeping bag before you need it. Always shake out clothing and footwear before putting them on.

Kissing bugs, also known as conenose bugs, are obnoxious insects that live in rodent nests and feed on mammal blood at night, leaving a large, itchy welt on the victim. They are not a problem during the cooler months, but during the warmer half of the year, they give desert backpackers one more reason to sleep in a fully closed net tent.

Ticks occur rarely in the desert. Do a careful full-body search every day if you see ticks. It is important to remove embedded ticks before they have a chance to transmit disease, which takes a day or more.

Other insects such as bees, velvet ants, and wasps give painful but nonthreatening stings. The exception is for people who have a known allergic reaction to specific insect stings. Since the reaction can develop rapidly and be life threatening, such people should carry insect sting kits prescribed by their doctors.

A new hazard has recently appeared in the Southwest, the **Africanized bee or killer bee.** These honeybees were accidentally introduced into Brazil in the 1950s and have since spread north to Texas and Arizona. They're expected to continue spreading across the warmer deserts. Because of their tropical origins, Africanized bees are sensitive to cold and will not likely become numerous in higher desert mountains and plateaus. It is possible that a hiker could encounter Africanized bees in lower desert areas. Popularly known as killer bees, they have been responsible for about 1,000 human deaths in the Western Hemisphere but only a few deaths in the United States. The hazard to a person who is allergic to bee stings is obvious. However, every documented fatal case in the Western Hemisphere has involved an allergic individual or someone who was infirm or otherwise unable to escape. I have yet to hear of any serious encounters between Africanized bees and hikers. Although the Africanized bee's venom is no more toxic than the common European honeybees, they are more aggressive in defending their hives and will sometimes swarm or chase an intruder.

European honeybees cause about 100 deaths per year in the United Sates.

⋘

Avoid all beehives. This includes cultivated bees, which may be a mixture of both types. Cultivated beehives are stacks of white boxes always found near roads. Wild bees build hives in rock crevices, holes in trees, and other protected places. Always avoid swarming bees. If attacked, protect your eyes and run away (drop your pack if necessary). Do not swat the bees; Africanized bees react aggresively. If shelter such as a tent, car, or building is available, use it. Africanized bees apparently don't pursue more than half a mile.

⋘

Many scary-looking desert insects are **not dangerous.** Millipedes, whip scorpions, Jerusalem crickets, sun spiders, and tarantulas are examples of ferocious-looking creatures that are not a threat to humans.

HAZARDOUS PLANTS

Never eat any plant, unless you are an expert at identification and know what you're doing.

⋘

Dry, rocky areas may have **stinging nettles,** a broad, low plant with coarsely haired leaves. Contact may cause severe itching.

⋘

Poison ivy grows seasonally along streams and moister drainages in some desert areas. The oil found on the leaves and stems causes a severe skin reaction in many people. It has shiny, green leaves, which grow in groups of three. Avoid touching posion ivy plants as well as walking sticks or other items that you suspect may have been exposed to poison ivy. The oil can persist on inanimate objects. If you accidentally come into contact with poison ivy or suspect you have, wash the affected skin with water as soon as you can. This will deactivate the oil before the skin has a chance to absorb it. **Calamine lotion** can help relieve the itching if you do have a skin reaction.

Slow-growing desert plants have developed an interesting array of defenses to protect themselves and their precious moisture from animals, birds, and insects that would like to dine on them. Spines and thorns are some of the obvious features of cacti and cactus-like plants. Most spines are needle-like, and an encounter results in a simple puncture. Warm southern deserts, such as the Sonoran, have most of the cacti and thorny plants; the cold northern deserts, such as the Great Basin, have scratchy plants such as sage and only a few types of cacti.

Teddy bear cholla of the Sonoran Desert looks cute and cuddly. It's not. Each branch has thousands of slender spines, each with invisible barbs, which attach themselves to people so easily the plant is sometimes called jumping cholla. If a burr sticks to your skin or clothing, remove it with a pocket comb or a pair of sticks. Then use a good pair of tweezers to pick out the remaining spines. If the spines become deeply imbedded, the victim should seek medical attention. When walking though a cholla field, watch the ground carefully. Most species of chollas have fragile joints that break off easily. The ground around the plants is usually littered with fallen joints, and their spines retain their microscopic barbs until they decay.

Use care around plants with large, spine-tipped leaves such as the **agaves and yuccas.** The spines can cause deep puncture wounds if you accidentally stumble into them or grab one as a handhold. The edges of the stiff leaves often have hooked thorns that can cause nasty scratches or deeper wounds.

Some **small cacti,** such as the aptly named pincushion cactus, are small, straw colored, and tend to hide in grass. They are a particular hazard when scrambling up rocky areas.

Catclaw is a bush that sometimes grows in dense thickets. The sharp, curved thorns catch on clothing and skin, and have to be carefully peeled off. Long-sleeved shirts and pants help, but it's best to avoid the thickets altogether.

BLISTERS

Wearing two pairs of socks—a thin inner and heavy outer—can reduce friction on your skin and cut down on blisters (see page 23 for additional suggestions).

Pay special attention to the **fit of new boots,** and always take them on a few trial day hikes and shorter backpack trips before committing to a long trip. Even though lightweight fabric-and-leather boots require little break-in, you still want to be sure of the fit.

At the first sign of a **hot spot** or other discomfort on your feet, stop and have a look. Protect a hot spot with a piece of felt moleskin. Changing to clean socks will help as well. Once a blister has fully developed, protect it with a piece of moleskin with the center cut out to surround the raised area of skin.

HOT WEATHER

During the summer, **hot weather is a serious hazard.** The lower desert areas may reach temperatures of 115 degrees F, and dehydration, heat exhaustion, and heat stroke are real possibilities. Don't underestimate the consequences of running out of water. Each hiker needs as much as 2 gallons of water every day. When temperatures exceed 100 degrees F, a person can survive only a day or two without water.

Even when water is plentiful and the weather moderate, **dehydration** can still be a problem. Even a slight loss of body fluid decreases your mental and physical abilities, and increases your susceptibility to heat-related medical problems.

In very hot weather, it's safer to hike in **higher, cooler areas** or to do hikes that follow streams.

Always **drink the water you have**—your body will use it efficiently. Conserving water is a poor plan and leads to dehydration. Your body can lose significant amounts of moisture without sweating and without becoming thirsty. Drink more water than required to quench your thirst.

Many **sport drinks replace electrolytes,** which are essential to processing the water you drink.

If stranded or low on water in hot weather, **conserve your sweat.** Rest in the shade during the day—this reduces your water needs by one-half or more. Travel during morning and evening, or at night when the air is cooler.

COLD WEATHER

Snow may fall at any time of year on the higher desert mountain ranges. Be prepared by bringing more warm clothing than you think you will need. During the cooler season, wear synthetic garments made of polypropylene or polyester fibers. These fibers retain their insulating ability when wet better than any natural fiber, including wool.

Avoid continuous exposure to chilling weather, which may subtly lower body temperature and cause collapse from **hypothermia,** a life-threatening condition. The insidious heat loss caused by cool winds, especially with rain, is the most dangerous. Hypothermia is a hazard especially in wet canyon bottoms, especially during spring and late fall. If the air is cool as well as the water, you may want to plan the hike for a warmer time of year. You can completely prevent hypothermia by adjusting your **clothing layers** to keep yourself comfortably warm, and by eating and drinking regularly so that your body produces heat to replace that which is lost.

FLASH FLOODS

Heavy rain can occur suddenly in the desert, especially during late summer when thunderstorms often form. Several inches of rain can easily fall in a small area within a few minutes. Because vegetation is sparse, runoff is rapid, and the water gathers force as it collects into the main drainages. The resulting flood often contains as much sand, gravel, rocks, and other debris as it does water, and may travel for miles from the place where the rain fell.

Never camp or park a vehicle in a dry wash or drainage. You may never hear or see the storm that causes the wash to flash flood.

If you're in a drainage when water does start to flow or the existing flow starts to increase, immediately **get to higher ground,** abandoning equipment if you have to. The main flood can arrive with very little warning.

❦

Never cross a flooded area, either on foot or by vehicle. The water is usually muddy and turbulent, which makes it impossible to gauge its depth. Just ankle-deep water can sweep you off your feet and only a foot of water can sweep a vehicle downstream.

❦

Flash floods are especially **dangerous in narrow canyons** where the high walls prevent an escape. Plan these hikes during periods of stable weather only.

❦

Be aware of the seasonal and long-term **weather patterns** in your hiking area. If it's a local area, learn the weather patterns, and keep an eye on them before your trip. If you plan to hike in a distant area, check with the land managers for the degree of flash flood hazard.

❦

Get the **extended weather forecast** from the National Weather Service just before leaving civilization.

Flood debris in narrow canyon

LIGHTNING

Thunderstorms can occur any month of the year in the Southwest, even with snowstorms, but they are most common during late summer. If a thunderstorm threatens, get off high ridges and peaks. Don't camp on ridges or exposed areas during active thunderstorm periods.

IF LIGHTNING CATCHES YOU
1. **Discard metal objects** such as climbing gear or metal walking sticks.
2. **Crouch on the ground** with your feet close together.
3. Use **something insulating** such as a sleeping pad between you and the ground, if possible.
4. **Don't touch the ground** with your hands when lightning is nearby. Most lightning injuries are not caused by the direct strike, but by the ground currents that spread out in every direction from the strike. Minimizing your contact with the ground reduces your exposure to the currents.
5. **Don't take shelter under lone trees** or in shallow caves.
6. It is also a good idea for people in groups to **spread out,** so that someone will be unaffected by a strike and be able to administer first aid.

LEAVE NO TRACE

The desert is fragile, though it gives an initial impression of being a tough landscape. Widely spaced plants and elusive wildlife are adapted to unforgiving climate conditions and often have a tenuous hold on life. If scarred, the desert takes a long time to recover. With a little care and common sense, we desert hikers can minimize the damage we do.

Don't disturb animals or destroy plants.

Don't disturb old ruins, rock drawings, or artifacts, whether made by Native Americans or immigrant prospectors. State and federal law protects these sites, and if left undisturbed, they can provide important clues to human and natural history.

If you're following a trail, stay on it. Don't cut switchbacks or take other shortcuts. Desert trails don't receive much maintenance, so shortcuts tend to become false trails. False trails can mislead other hikers and cause erosion. Moreover, as experienced hikers know, shortcutting uses more energy than staying on the trail.

Groups should **spread out when hiking** cross-country instead of walking single file, to avoid creating trails.

When traveling cross-country, **hike on less-fragile areas** as much as is practical. Gravel wash bottoms form good routes, for example. In canyon country, you can often follow rock outcrops and terraces.

✢

Many hikers own dogs and like to take them hiking. **Be considerate of wildlife** and other hikers by following any local regulations. **Keep your dog under control** and minimize barking.

✢

Most **dogs don't get along with cholla cactus.** One experience with removing the barbed spines from the paws and mouth of a very unhappy pet is usually enough to convince people to leave the dog at home.

✢

Cryptobiotic soil is the black, crusty layer that often forms on the surface in sandy areas. It's a combination of mosses, lichens, and bacteria that live together in an interdependent relationship and binds the sandy soil together. The crust takes many years to re-form once disturbed. Avoid cryptobiotic soil wherever possible and stay on the sandy areas between or on bedrock.

✢

Sound carries a long way in the open desert. **Respect other hikers'** desire for solitude by avoiding loud conversations and noise. Choose pack and clothing colors that blend in to the muted colors of the desert.

Some desert trails, such as those in the Grand Canyon, traverse very steep terrain with drop-offs. When **meeting pack animals** on steep terrain, move to the downhill side of the trail, or to the outside of bends or switchbacks, and stand quietly. Spooked animals can endanger themselves and their riders. Always follow instructions given by the packer.

Since **mountain bikes** are less maneuverable than hikers, move off the trail for them. This avoids making the cyclist ride off-trail, which creates tire ruts in fragile desert soil.

When **human waste** disposal is involved, desert country poses some special challenges for those who want to be considerate wilderness users. There's less open water to contaminate, but human waste decomposes very slowly in dry, sandy soil. If bathroom facilities are available (at trailheads and campgrounds, for example), use them. Otherwise, select a site at least 100 yards from streams, lakes, springs, and dry washes. If possible, avoid barren, sandy soil. Dig a small "cat-hole" about six inches down into the organic layer of the soil. When finished, refill the hole, making the site as natural as possible.

Land managers now recommend that you carry out all toilet paper and, in some heavily used areas, all human waste as well. Carry **used toilet paper** and other hygiene items in doubled zipper bags, with a small amount of baking soda to absorb odor.

A **small plastic trowel** makes it easier to dig holes and minimize damage to ground cover.

PICKING YOUR CAMPSITE

To help preserve your own sense of wildness and that of others, choose a campsite **out of sight of other campers and hikers.** If you've been following a trail, move a couple of hundred yards away from it, and use rock outcrops, low ridges, or brush to block the view in that direction.

Avoid campsites near rock piles, old buildings, pack rat nests, or other piles of debris. These are favorite sites for rodents who may decide your presence signals a free dinner, and worse, for rattlesnakes who feast on the rodents. Insects are also more common in such areas.

Don't camp near desert water sources unless you can't avoid it (in a narrow canyon, for example). Animals usually move to water at night, and your presence may prevent them from getting a much-needed drink. In addition, the area around springs and natural water tanks tend to be overused. In Arizona, there's actually a state law that prohibits camping near a spring. Consider, too, that mice and other camp robbers are more numerous near water.

Learn to dry camp. Camping dry will open up many superb campsites, such as rimrock areas, ridges, and even mountain peaks. To avoid having to carry a heavy load of water all day, plan to pass a reliable water source during late afternoon. Pick up enough water to camp and to reach the next reliable water source the next day. Start looking for a campsite whenever you feel like it and camp wherever you like.

Camp on **ground that resists damage.** Sand, gravel, and rock ledges are excellent choices. As tempting as it might be, don't camp in desert flower fields or meadows during the wet season. Also, avoid cryptobiotic soil.

You'll want a reasonably level tent or bed site, but don't excavate one. You may be able to find small level sites on the **uphill sides of trees or boulders.**

If rain or stormy weather threatens, **pick a well-drained campsite.** A gentle slope, or slightly dome-shaped area keeps water from pooling under your tent.

Look for absorbent ground, such as pine needles (there are trees in many desert mountain ranges!), sand, or gravel. Never dig drainage ditches around your campsite—this outdated practice causes too much damage to soil and slow-growing vegetation.

Never camp in dry washes or drainages below the flood level, even in apparently stable weather. Heavy rain falling miles away can turn your camp into a deadly torrent with very little warning. At best, you'll lose all your gear, and at worst, you may lose your life.

In warm weather, you may wish to site your camp so it is **in the shade** as long as possible in the morning. In cold weather, you'll probably want the sun to hit your frosty tent or sleeping bag as early as possible. Check the direction of the sunrise on the first morning of your trip, then site your later camps appropriately.

Before leaving, **restore your campsite** to the natural condition it was in before your visit. Carefully look for bits of litter and gear you may have dropped or forgotten. Use a dead piece of brush to whisk over your tracks.

GO WITHOUT FIRE

Campfires are part of the wilderness experience for many hikers. Unfortunately, **fires should not be part of the desert experience**—there simply isn't enough wood. A responsible hiker should not build fires with scarce wood supplies. Land managers close some areas to campfires.

During periods of high fire danger, **campfires may be illegal.** Before your trip, check with the agency that manages your hiking area to see if any fire restrictions are in effect.

KEEPING FOOD FROM NIGHT VISITORS

Avoid heavily used campsites when possible. At these sites, camp-robber animals are used to humans and their food. Your arrival is the ringing of the dinner bell. At one desert campsite, a large, fearless skunk greeted my friend and I within minutes of our arrival. He walked right up to us as we were laying out our groundsheets, and it seemed to us that he had "Feed me!" written all over his face. We picked up our packs and hiked for another hour by headlamp rather than spend a sleepless night fending him off.

Never feed wild animals. Human food is not good for them, and they become dependent on handouts. Then they start to seek out human food and become camp robbers.

If you have trees in your campsite, **hang your food sacks** from a 10- or 15-foot high tree limb, if possible. The foolproof technique is to divide your food into two equal sacks. Use a stone to toss the end of a piece of nylon cord over the limb well out from the trunk, then tie half your food to the end. Pull the food up to the limb, and then tie your remaining food sack onto the cord as high as you can reach. Stuff the excess cord into the food sack, then use a stick to push the second sack several feet higher than your head. The first sack will act as a counterweight and descend a few feet, but it should remain at least as high as the second sack. In the morning, use a stick to pull down one of the sacks. This method is successful against most animals, even bears, if the sacks are at least 10 feet above the ground. However, any height you can achieve is better than leaving your food on the ground.

If there aren't any trees, look for a **couple of boulders** you can use to support a length of nylon cord horizontally.

The **top of a single boulder** can support a horizontal hiking stick or branch, extended into the air on one side. Weight the end of the stick with stones or jam it into a crack. Next, hang your food bags from the projecting end.

Hanging food bags

A party of three or more hikers can use walking sticks to **make a tripod** by lashing the tops together with cord. Since mice and other rodents can easily climb the sticks, hang your food bags low enough to be well away from the legs, but high enough so that animals can't jump onto the sacks.

If there's nothing at all to hang your food from, then you may have no choice but to **leave it in your pack.** Close all the plastic food bags to minimize odor, but leave the stuff sack open. Leave all the zippers and closures open on your pack, so mice won't chew a hole trying to get in. With luck, you'll only lose one or two of the more enticing items in your pack. Actually, if you camp in areas with little use, chances are you won't be bothered at all. Truly wild animals are very shy about approaching a human camp; usually you won't have problems unless you camp in the same site for several days.

BREAKING CAMP

Everything you carry into wild areas, you must also carry out.

At home, repackage your food into **resealable, zipper-locked bags** to minimize the amount of trash created on the trip.

Never bury food scraps, packaging, or any sort of trash. Animals will dig up anything with a food odor, and in the dry climate, trash lasts just about forever.

Never burn trash in a campfire. Many packaging materials contain thin layers of aluminum, which do not burn in even the hottest campfire. Like plastic, it fuses into small blobs. Old fire pits scar popular camping areas and glitter with bits of aluminum and plastic. In addition, some plastics give off highly toxic fumes when burned.

Carry out trash left by others. This is especially practical toward the end of your trip when your pack is light. Then you can bask in the glow of self-righteous pleasure!

Appendix A

SUGGESTED READING

Fletcher, Colin. *Complete Walker III.* New York: Alfred A. Knopf, 1984.

Harmon, Will. *Leave No Trace: Minimum Impact Outdoor Recreation.* Helena, Mont.: Falcon Publishing Co., 1997.

———. *Wild Country Companion.* Helena, Mont.: Falcon Publishing Co., 1994.

Larson, Peggy. *The Deserts of the Southwest: A Sierra Club Naturalists Guide.* San Francisco: Sierra Club Books, 1977.

Preston, Gilbert. *Wilderness First Aid.* Helena, Mont.: Falcon Publishing Co., 1997.

Appendix B

SAMPLE BACKPACKING CHECKLIST

Below is a checklist for one person on a seven-day backpack trip. As mentioned previously, solo hiking is not recommended, but each person in a group would likely carry similar items to the checklist below and share heavier cook gear, tent/tarp equipment, first-aid supplies, and water filtration equipment. The following checklist is for a specific trip. A hot-weather trip without water would warrant a different checklist. Use this checklist as an example only. Different trip conditions require different gear lists.

Trip conditions: Seven-day backpack trip, trail and cross-country, high temperatures in 80s F; several water sources most days with none on the third and fourth days, so 2 gallons of water will be carried leaving camp on the third day.

ITEM	WEIGHT (IN OUNCES)
Accessories	
1 altimeter/watch	1.3
1 comb	0.4
1 eyeglasses retainer	0.4
1 monocular w/case	3.2
1 paperback book	8.0

Clothing	
1 bandana	1.2
1 down jacket (Feathered Friends)	17.0
1 pair gloves, light fleece	1.3
1 hat, fleece	1.6
1 waterproof and windproof rain jacket	15.0
1 pair waterproof and windproof rain pants	13.1
1 pair shorts	5.5
1 pair socks, spare set (polypropylene liners and wool outer)	5.7
1 lightweight thermal underwear top	7.2
1 underwear top, polypropylene, expedition weight	15.0
Emergency	
1 first aid/repair/snake kit	20.0
Essentials	
4 AA alkaline batteries	3.6
1 compass	2.0
1 headlamp w/alkaline battery	3.5
1 insect repellent, 2 oz.	4.0
4 maps, USGS 7.5 quad	5.0
1 sun hat	3.0
1 sunscreen, 4 oz.	5.3
1 roll toilet paper	7.0
2 qts. water	64.0
1 pair sunglasses	negligible
Kitchen	
1 oz. baking soda	1.0
1 coffee filter holder, modified	1.5
1 1.5-cup-capacity stainless steel drinking cup	3.0
1 dental floss	0.5
1 dozen coffee filters	0.5
2 food stuffsacks	2.0
7 days food (1 lb. 10 oz./day)	182.0
1 handiwipe/potcleaner	0.5
2 bottles iodine tablets, 50 tablets each	2.4

1 kitchen ditty bag	0.5
3 lighters, large	2.7
1 pot, 1 qt. stainless steel w/lid	7.5
1 potgripper, aluminum	1.4
1 salt dispenser (plastic bottle)	1.5
1 bottle liquid biodegradable soap	0.5
2 spoons	0.5
2 stove fuel containers, 7 oz. net	24.0
1 stove	5.5
1 toothbrush	0.5
1 2-gal. water bag	3.0
1 1-qt. water bottle	4.0
Pack	
1 pocket knife	2.7
1 pack	112.0
1 large raincover (Gregory)	6.5
Photography	
2 batteries	2.0
6 rolls film, 135-36	6.0
1 lens paper	0.5
1 notebook	1.4
1 camera w/film	11.0
1 pencil	0.3
Sleeping	
1 groundsheet, 4 x 9 feet, 3 mil. plastic, w/sack	8.5
1 sleeping bag, w/stuffsack	34.5
1 tarp, 10 x 8 feet, with stakes and cord	26.5
1 sleeping pad, 3/4 length	25.0
Total Weight	***695.2 ounces or 43.4 pounds***

About the Author

Bruce Grubbs has been hiking and exploring the American deserts for more than thirty years. He is the author of five other FalconGuides—*Hiking Northern Arizona, Hiking Nevada, Hiking Oregon's Three Sisters Country, Hiking Great Basin National Park,* and *Hiking Arizona* (with Stewart Aitchison). He lives in Flagstaff, Arizona.

Notes

Notes

Notes

FALCONGUIDES® are available for where-to-go hiking, mountain biking, rock climbing, walking, scenic driving, fishing, rockhounding, paddling, birding, wildlife viewing, and camping. We also have FalconGuides on essential outdoor skills and subjects and field identification. The following titles are currently available, but this list grows every year. For a free catalog with a complete list of titles, call FALCON toll-free at 1-800-582-2665.

Mountain Biking Guides 

Mountain Biking Arizona
Mountain Biking Colorado
Mountain Biking Georgia
Mountain Biking New Mexico
Mountain Biking New York
Mountain Biking Northern New England
Mountain Biking Oregon
Mountain Biking South Carolina
Mountain Biking Southern New England
Mountain Biking Utah
Mountain Biking Wisconsin

Local Cycling Series

Fat Trax Bozeman
Fat Trax Colorado Springs
Mountain Biking Bend
Mountain Biking Boise
Mountain Biking Chequamegon
Mountain Biking Denver/Boulder
Mountain Biking Durango
Mountain Biking Helena
Mountain Biking Moab
Mountain Biking White Mountains

■ *To order any of these books, check with your local bookseller or call FALCON® at* ***1-800-582-2665***.

www.falconguide.com

FALCON®